For the wild swans of Slimbridge

Text copyright © 1985 by Jonathan Cape Ltd.
Illustrations copyright © 1985 by Deborah King.
First published in Great Britain in 1985 by Jonathan Cape Ltd.

Printed in Italy by New Interlitho, SpA, Milan

First U.S. Edition
1 2 3 4 5 6 7 8 9 10

Library of Congress Cataloging in Publication Data

Lewis, Naomi.
    Swan.
    Summary: Presents the physical characteristics and habits of the Bewick swan, one of the smallest and rarest of swans, describing its mating on the Arctic tundra in the spring and its long migration to the south for the winter.
    1. Bewick's swan—Juvenile literature. [1. Bewick's swan. 2. Swans] I. King, Deborah, ill. II. Title.
QL696.A52L48 1986   598.4'1   85–15961
ISBN 0–688–05534–6
ISBN 0–688–05535–4 (lib. bdg.)

DEBORAH KING

SWAN

Story told by Naomi Lewis

LOTHROP, LEE & SHEPARD BOOKS   NEW YORK

ONE morning, late in April, a wild swan lands on the vast wastes of the Arctic tundra, the breeding place of his kind. He is a Bewick's swan, smallest and rarest of the swans in the northern hemisphere. It is nearly two months since he left the Severn Estuary to make the journey north with other wild swans. But he flew apart, a bird of sorrow. Several years ago his mate of many seasons died in a storm over the Baltic Sea. They had raised numbers of young swans on the tundra, and some of these were with him on the flight.

This spring his life will change, for among the new arrivals is a female swan who also has no mate.

THEY rise together in the water, touching breasts and bobbing their heads. They call to each other softly. The two swans have little time for courting, since the Arctic spring and summer are so short. And in those few months the new young birds must be hatched and made strong enough for the long return flight south – a distance of some 2,600 miles. To balance the long winter of frozen soil and total darkness, the Arctic summer is a marvel of light and colour and birdsong. The brilliant sun dissolves the ice on the river, lake and shore; flowers and grasses spring from the warmed earth; the unpolluted waters are a dazzling green and blue.

Only a few birds stay through the year and know the Arctic night. These are the ptarmigan, the gyrfalcon and the snowy owl, who now is obliged to hunt in daylight, and finds it hard.

A STRONG bond has quickly grown between the swan and his new mate. He takes her to a quiet place near a lake where his earlier families were raised, and together they build a flood-proof mound of reeds and moss. On the top of this the female makes a hollow, which she lines with feathers and down. There she lays five large, off-white eggs. They must be kept warm, so she rarely leaves them. After some thirty days the first egg hatches, two days later the next, until after ten days five cygnets are safely born. They are pale grey and fluffy, with bright eyes and soft voices, and they take to the water at once. The tops of their bills are reddish-purple, which will turn to yellow by next summer.

The parents help the little swans to feed by loosening roots of waterweed, and by treading the mud of shallow water to bring small insects to the surface. Soon the cygnets have learnt to look for food themselves. They swim close to their parents, calling in their soft trilling voices, somersaulting and diving through the reeds. And they learn very early to preen themselves; this activates the oil gland which waterproofs their feathers.

THE cob, or male swan, stays nearby, alert to keep off predators – a raven or a fox. One day an Arctic fox ventures near the nest. The cob turns on him with fearsome cries, and outstretched neck and wings; terrified, the fox retreats. But man, the worst of all their enemies, has not so far invaded their Arctic breeding grounds.

BY July the young birds are expert feeders and have learnt the useful skill of up-ending – diving down from the surface for food. All through August the birds prepare for the long flight south. The adults moult their feathers, and while the new ones are growing they must keep to the ground. As the days shorten, the birds feel restless. Geese and ducks circle overhead, their voices filling the air. The swans begin to wander, losing all former ties with their territory. The parents anxiously try to keep their young together.

One late afternoon in September, when the sky is clear and the wind is light, a melodious trumpeting sounds overhead. A flock of swans is leaving for the south. The cob listens, rises into the air, and calls to his family to follow. More and more birds leave in the coming days; the light dwindles and soon the tundra is left to its dark and ice and mystery.

IT is almost dusk when the swans begin their journey, and they fly on through the night. We can see why these are the birds of fairy-tale. The moon and stars, the rising and the setting sun are their continual guides. Three families always group together with the male at the head of each, the whole forming a V-shaped wedge; the young ones are helped by flying in the slipstream of the stronger birds ahead. The cob is a very experienced bird, leading them high above the clouds. Sometimes, in a heavy storm, they rise as much as five miles above the ground. But this is dangerous since ice may clog their wings. The average speed of the flock is fifty miles an hour; with a strong wind behind them they can reach seventy.

But they try to cover as much as 300 miles before they stop, and go down to one of their familiar landing places, by marsh or lake or grassland, where they can rest and feed.

A GOOD wind has been behind the flock, and since their last descent they have crossed another 300 miles. But they need to rest and feed, the young especially, and the cob steers his group to a place that he knows well, a small shallow lake on the edge of marshlands. There, using their special trick of up-ending, they dive for the rich underwater vegetation. The cygnets cannot dislodge the valuable starchy roots by themselves; that needs the strength of adult birds. So the parents loosen the plants with their feet, then pull them out with their bills.

B UT not every place of refuge can be trusted. Lake Ladoga, to the south of the Arctic, has long been a favourite with travelling birds, and when they reach it the cob leads his flock to a quiet corner, shaded over with trees. But something keeps him from settling; all through the night he is anxious and alert. At sunrise the air crackles with gunfire. Swans, ducks and geese rise up in panic and so become easy targets. The cob at last collects his flock and they fly to another shelter, an estuary where they are left in peace. Here they stay for several days, to rest their wings and recover strength.

So the flight continues.

THE birds are never out of danger. Freezing cold and exhaustion cause the death of two of the five cygnets. Other young birds in the flock collide with overhead wires. Some even fly into trees and buildings – strange objects which these tundra-born young could not have learnt to avoid. Worst of all enemies is the human with the gun. More than a third of the total number of swans returning to the sanctuary are found to have shot in their tissues. Others are slowly poisoned by lead pellets, left from shooting and fishing, swallowed by the birds in mistake for gravel.

Still many birds survive. And early one November morning the melodious call of returning Bewick's swans can be heard in the sky. The cob and his flock touch down. They are in sanctuary.

THEY know this place, "Swan Lake" in Slimbridge, as a safe and welcoming site. As the weeks pass the cob sees more of his kind arrive. The earlier comers greet the late arrivers with bobbing heads and flapping wings, and the cob is joined by offspring of his own from former years. They are now fully grown, but not all are parents yet. These swans are long-lived birds, and though they may find partners before that time, they do not start to breed until they are four or five years old.

SPACE is sometimes short as the numbers grow, and one male bird is rash enough to encroach on the cob's home area. The two birds raise their wings and arch their snake-like necks in angry combat, while the females watch, keeping a discreet distance from the battle. The cob soon routs the interloper, and peace returns.

AT first the tired flocks are content to feed on the grass and underwater plants and weeds. The yellow cress which grows on the shoreline is a particular delicacy. The Bewick's swan is more agile on land than the larger kinds, the mute or the whooper, so the cob and his family begin to roam the fields, where they may find sprouting grain or potatoes left to rot. Other wild swans join them, and as they wander the wind carries their musical babble far over the fens and fields of this flat region. But the last of the autumn mildness soon is gone. When the first snow falls on the icy marshes the birds gather together for warmth and protection against the bitter wind.

THE winter is severe this year. In January and February the marshes are often frozen hard, and the swans must fly further afield in their search for food. Most of the nearby lakes and waterways are covered with ice; if the birds land too hastily they skid and slide along on their tails until they can right themselves. The cob, and other adult birds, know how to do this with proper dignity. But the cygnets are baffled by the slippery surface; they fall forwards on to their bills, tails in the air; they spin round in circles. Other swans and geese accept the situation. They place their heads under their wings and wait for the thaw.

THE parent swans and their three cygnets have now spent their first winter together. They have explored the rivers, estuaries and floodmeadows for miles around, and the young birds have a useful plan of the landscape in their minds for future years. For they will come again, and again. Now, at the restless end of March they must start their long flight to the tundra, where a new brood will be born. Standing in a field of winter wheat, they hear overhead the strange and thrilling call of the first swans travelling north. For this family of wild swans too, it is time to leave.

ON A perfectly still evening, the moon full in the sky lighting the way, the cob lifts off from the lake. Before long, the wild swans vanish with haunting cries into the unknown, to ride once more the currents of the cold north wind.

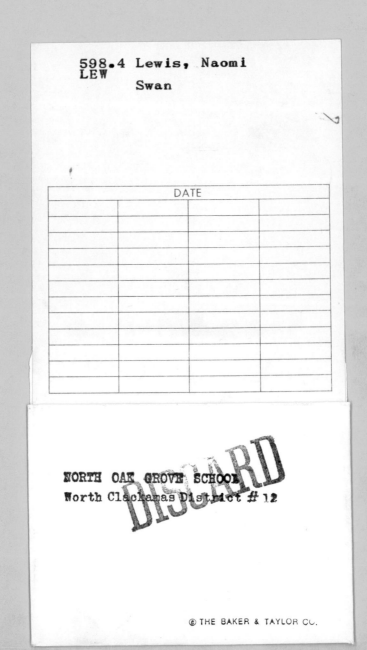

598.4 Lewis, Naomi
LEW
Swan

DATE			